Mine Hunting Ships

by Melissa Abramovitz

CAPSTONE
HIGH-INTEREST
BOOKS

an imprint of Capstone Press
Mankato, Minnesota

Capstone High-Interest Books are published by Capstone Press
151 Good Counsel Drive, P.O. Box 669, Mankato, Minnesota 56002
http://www.capstone-press.com

Library of Congress Cataloging-in-Publication Data
Abramovitz, Melissa, 1954-
    Mine hunting ships/by Melissa Abramovitz.
    p. cm.—(Land and sea)
    Includes bibliographical references (p. 44) and index.
    ISBN 0-7368-0758-6
    1. Minesweepers—Juvenile literature. [1. Minesweepers.] I. Title. II. Land and sea
(Mankato, Minn.)
V856 .A26 2001
359.8'362—dc21   00-010266

Summary: Describes the history, design, weapons, and missions of mine hunting ships.

Editorial Credits
Carrie A. Braulick, editor; James Franklin, cover designer; Timothy Halldin,
    production designer and illustrator; Katy Kudela, photo researcher

Photo Credits
Defense Visual Information Center, cover, 7, 8, 16, 33, 36, 39, 40, 43, 46
NHF Historical Services, 18, 20, 22
North Wind Picture Archives, 12
Photri-Microstock, 10, 24, 27, 34–35
Robert Rathe/FPG International LLC, 4, 31

**Special thanks to Public Affairs Officer Lt. Chuck Bell, Mine Warfare Command,
for his assistance in preparing this book.**

1 2 3 4 5 6 06 05 04 03 02 01

Table of Contents

Mine Hunting Ships

Militaries often use mines in warfare. Aircraft, submarines, and ships often plant mines underwater. These explosives are designed to destroy enemy ships. The U.S. Navy uses mine hunting ships to locate, identify, and neutralize underwater mines. Neutralized mines can no longer explode and harm ships.

Mines

Mines are classified according to their position in the water. Bottom mines are placed on the ocean floor. Moored mines are attached to a cable. The cable is attached to an anchor on the ocean floor. They float at a certain depth.

Mine hunting ships are designed to locate and neutralize underwater mines.

Mines also are classified according to how they explode. Contact mines explode when an object hits them. Other mines are influence mines. Influence mines can explode without being hit by an object.

Influence mines include magnetic, acoustic, and pressure mines. Magnetic mines explode when they sense a ship's magnetism. This force attracts metal. Acoustic mines explode when they detect a ship's sounds. Pressure mines sense water pressure. Large ships push down on the water. This pressure then makes the mines explode.

Mine Hunting

Mine hunting ships are able to find and neutralize mines. Both warships and merchant ships depend on mine hunting ships to keep them safe from mines. Merchant ships are used for trade and business.

The Navy's mine hunting ships include coastal minehunters (MHCs) and mine countermeasures ships (MCMs). MHCs locate

Contact mines explode when an object touches them.

MHCs neutralize one mine at a time.

and neutralize one mine at a time. They use sonar to find mines. This device bounces sound waves off objects to locate them.

MCMs also have sonar to find individual mines. But MCMs include equipment called sweeps. The sweeps have cables that neutralize mines in a large area. These sweeps can be mechanical or influence sweeps.

Mechanical sweeps have a cable with cutters. The sweeps cut the cables of moored mines. The mines then float to the water's surface. A diver then places a small explosive on the mines to make them safely explode.

Influence sweeps create a magnetic field that explodes influence mines. These sweeps also may make ship sounds to make these mines explode. Some influence sweeps cancel a ship's magnetism. Crewmembers aboard mine hunting ships make sure they explode mines a safe distance away from the ships.

Classes and Features

The Navy groups its ships into classes. All ships in a class have similar features. The Navy's 12 MHCs make up the *Osprey* class. MHCs are 188 feet (57 meters) long. Their displacement is 893 tons (810 metric tons). Displacement is the weight of the water that would fill the space taken up by the ship. MHCs have a top speed of 10 knots. One knot equals about 1.15 miles (1.85 kilometers) per hour. MHCs have two machine guns.

The Navy's 14 MCMs are in the *Avenger* class. These ships are 224 feet (68 meters) long. They have a displacement of 1,312 tons (1,190 metric tons). Their top speed is 14 knots. MCMs also have two machine guns.

The Navy has 14 MCMs in the *Avenger* class.

Chapter Two

History

David Bushnell invented the first sea mine in 1776. It was called the Bushnell keg mine. He made this contact mine from a keg filled with gunpowder. The U.S. military first used keg mines in combat during the Revolutionary War (1775–1783). The American colonies fought against Great Britain during this war.

The U.S. military placed keg mines in the Delaware River to destroy British ships. This river forms the eastern border of Delaware. But two boys were killed when they touched the mines. The British learned about the mines after this accident. They then destroyed all of the mines by shooting them.

The U.S. military began to use Bushnell keg mines in the late 1700s.

The Civil War

During the Civil War (1861–1865), the United States and the Confederate States of America fought against each other. Southern states made up the Confederate States of America.

During the war, the Confederate Navy used Bushnell keg mines against the U.S. Navy. The mines hit 43 of the United States' ships. But two Confederate ships also hit mines after some mines drifted away.

World War I

During World War I (1914–1918), the Allies and the Central Powers often used underwater mines. The Central Powers included Germany, Bulgaria, Austria-Hungary, and Turkey. The Allies included the United States, Great Britain, France, Russia, Belgium, and Japan.

At this time, the only mine hunting ships were called minesweepers. These ships had mechanical or influence sweeps attached to them.

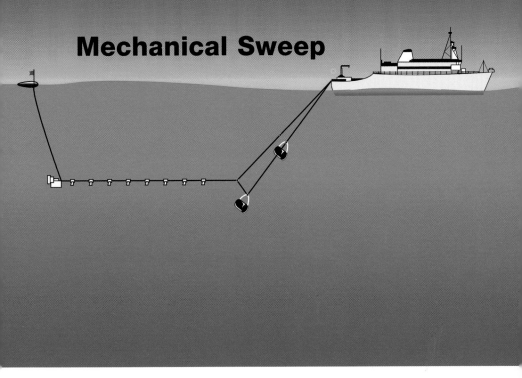

Mechanical Sweep

Both the Allies and Central Powers used minesweepers during World War I. The first minesweepers were built on fishing boat bases. These boats had a long cable attached to them to catch mines. Sailors sometimes used two minesweepers to cover a wider area. In 1917, a fisherman invented the Oropesa sweep. This mechanical sweep had a pair of cables to catch mines. It could catch more mines than earlier sweeps.

The Navy used acoustic and magnetic minesweepers during World War II.

The Allies and Central Powers began to use contact mines called antenna mines during the war. These mines were attached to a wire. The mines exploded when a ship touched any part of the wire. Earlier contact mines would not explode unless the ship hit the mine. Antenna mines were more difficult for ships to avoid.

World War II

Underwater mines damaged more ships than any other weapon during World War II (1939–1945). The Allied nations fought against the Axis powers during this war. The Allied nations included the United States, Great Britain, the Soviet Union, Canada, and France. The Axis powers included Germany, Italy, and Japan.

During the war, the Allied nations and Axis powers used contact, magnetic, acoustic, and pressure mines. The U.S. Navy neutralized magnetic mines in various ways. It designed the LL sweep. This influence sweep had two electric cables. An electric current passed along the cables. The current created a magnetic field. The mines exploded when they sensed the magnetic field.

Some ships used a degaussing system to avoid setting off magnetic mines. A thick band of electrical wires was located on the outside of the ship. A machine called a generator sent an

electric current through the wires. This charge canceled the ship's magnetism. The U.S. Navy built some World War II minesweepers of wood to protect them from magnetic mines. A magnetic force does not attract wood.

The Navy neutralized pressure mines by placing a large object such as a barge in the water above the mines. These large, flat-bottomed boats created enough water pressure to make the mines explode.

World War II Minesweepers

The Navy's minesweepers during World War II included ships in the DMS class. These ships were 314.5 feet (95.9 meters) long. They had a displacement of 1,060 to 1,190 tons (962 to 1,080 metric tons). DMS-class ships had a top speed of 32.5 knots. They carried five guns.

World War II minesweepers also included *Bird*-class ships. These ships were 188 feet (57 meters) long. They had a displacement of 840 tons (762 metric tons). *Bird*-class ships traveled at a top speed of 14 knots. They had two guns.

Many World War II minesweepers were made of wood.

The Navy also used *Raven/Auk* AM-class minesweepers during World War II. These ships were 221.5 feet (67.5 meters) long. They had a displacement of 810 to 890 tons (735 to 807 metric tons). *Raven/Auk* AM ships traveled at a top speed of 18 knots. They carried four or five guns.

The *Steady* was in the *Raven/Auk* AM class.

Chapter Three

Modern Mine Hunting Ships

After World War II, the Navy developed new mine hunting ships. It produced mine hunting ships that had no magnetic parts. The Navy also began to equip mine hunting ships with sonar equipment. This equipment helped ships locate mines.

The Korean War

During the Korean War (1950–1953), South Korea fought against North Korea. The United States fought alongside South Korea. In 1950, the North Korean military planted more than 3,000 mines in a port near the city of Wonsan,

The Navy used devices that made ship sounds to explode acoustic mines during the Korean War.

North Korea. These mines kept U.S. ships from entering the port for a week until minesweepers cleared the area. Several of these minesweepers were destroyed when they hit mines. Navy commanders then decided to improve their mine hunting ships.

The Navy built Minesweeper, Ocean (MSO) minesweepers. It made MSO ships with non-metal parts to avoid setting off magnetic mines. MSO ships could sweep for contact, acoustic, and magnetic mines. Most previous minesweepers only swept for contact mines. The Navy used MSO ships until 1994.

MSO ships were in one of three classes. These classes were *Aggressive*, *Agile*, and *Acme*. *Aggressive*- and *Agile*-class MSO ships were 172 feet (52 meters) long. They had a displacement of 853 tons (774 metric tons). They traveled at a top speed of 15 knots. These MSO ships had two machine guns.

Acme-class ships were 173 feet (53 meters) long. They had a displacement of 818 tons (742 metric tons). These ships traveled at a top

MSO minesweepers could sweep for contact, acoustic, and magnetic mines.

speed of 14 knots. *Acme*-class ships also had two machine guns.

The Vietnam War

During the Vietnam War (1954–1975), South Vietnam and North Vietnam fought against each other. The United States fought alongside South Vietnam.

The militaries involved in the Vietnam War used rivers to transport supplies and weapons. The North Vietnamese military planted mines in some of these rivers.

The Navy's minesweepers were designed for oceans. They did not fit on the small rivers. The Navy then built 13 minesweeping boats (MSBs) to clear the river mines. The MSBs were 57 feet (17 meters) long. During the war, these boats patrolled almost 3,000 miles (4,830 kilometers) on rivers in South Vietnam. After the war, the Navy gave many of these MSBs to the South Vietnamese Navy.

MCMs and MHCs

The U.S. Navy continued to improve its mine hunting ships. In 1987, the Navy started using MCMs. It began using MHCs in 1993.

The Navy began using MCMs in 1987.

MCM and MHC ships have several features to help them avoid being damaged by mines. They are built with many non-magnetic parts to avoid setting off magnetic mines. The engines on MCMs and MHCs have low-magnetic parts. These ships also have an advanced degaussing system to protect them from magnetic mines. MCM and MHC engines are designed to run quietly.

Gulf War Mine Operations

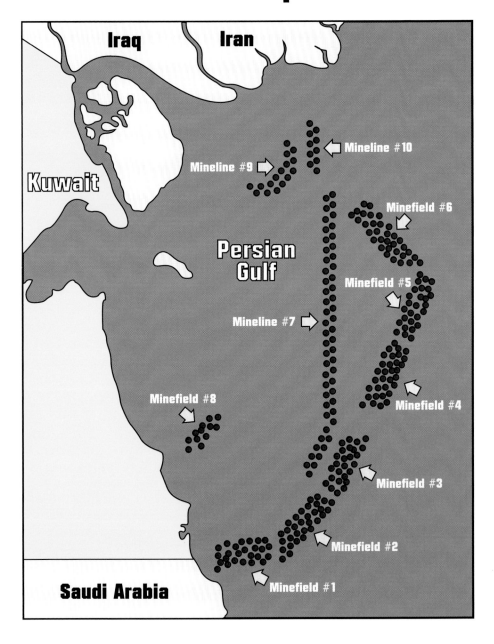

This feature helps them avoid activating acoustic mines.

MCMs and MHCs have non-metal hulls. The hull is a ship's main body. The ship's bow is located at the hull's front. Its stern is located at the hull's rear. MCMs have wooden hulls covered with fiberglass. This strong material is made of fine threads of glass. MHC hulls are made entirely of fiberglass.

The Navy used MCM ships in combat for the first time during the Gulf War (1991). This war started after Iraq invaded Kuwait. The U.S. military helped force Iraq's military out of Kuwait. The Navy's MCMs cleared more than 500 Iraqi mines in the Persian Gulf. This body of water surrounds Kuwait's and Iraq's coasts.

Locating Mines

MCMs and MHCs tow sonar to locate mines. These ships use the AN/SQQ-32 Advanced Mine Hunting Sonar. The AN/SQQ-32 is a variable depth sonar. It operates at many different water depths.

Large rocks or debris on the ocean floor can interfere with sonar. For this reason, MCMs have one mechanical sweep. This sweep is called the AN/SQL-36 Standard Mechanical Minesweep.

MCM ships also have an AN/SQL-37 Standard Magnetic/Acoustic Influence Minesweeping System. This system creates a magnetic field and ship sounds to explode magnetic and acoustic mines.

Mine Neutralization

MCMs and MHCs usually use the AN/SQL-48 Mine Neutralization System to neutralize mines. The main part of this system is a remote controlled Mine Neutralization Vehicle (MNV). This vehicle is 12 feet (3.7 meters) long and weighs 2,700 pounds (1,225 kilograms). The MNV is attached to the ship by a heavy cable.

When sonar detects a mine, crewmembers launch the MNV over the ship's side. Crewmembers use computers to give the MNV

MCMs and MHCs have a great deal of equipment to help them locate and neutralize mines.

commands. These commands are transferred through the cable. The commands tell the MNV how to reach the mine. The MNV also carries its own sonar and video systems to locate the mine.

After the MNV reaches the mine, the ship's crewmembers identify the type of mine. An AN/UYQ-31 video camera provides images to help the crew identify the mine. The MNV then places an explosive charge on or near the mine. Crewmembers use a remote control to explode the mine when the MNV is back on the ship.

MNVs were useful during the Gulf War. MCM crewmembers used them to safely neutralize mines on more than 120 missions.

Inchon

In the late 1990s, the Navy began using a mine countermeasures support ship. This ship is called the *Inchon*. The ship is 602 feet (183 meters) long. It has a displacement of 18,340 tons (16,638 metric tons). *Inchon* is an amphibious ship. This type of ship carries other ships and supplies from sea to land.

The *Inchon* carries supplies to mine hunting ships.

Inchon also is an aircraft carrier. Minesweeping helicopters can take off and land on its flight deck. These helicopters have mechanical sweeps attached to them. They can sweep for and cut underwater mines as ships do. *Inchon* brings supplies to mine hunting ships. It also is a repair center for mine hunting ships and minesweeping helicopters.

Radar Equipment

Bow

Fiberglass Hull

Main Propulsion Plant

Stern

Inflatable Boats

Chapter Four

The Future

Military experts believe that the world's militaries will continue to use mines for many years. The U.S. Navy must continue to improve its mine hunting ships to keep other ships safe.

Improving Communication Equipment

The Navy is improving communication systems between mine hunting ships and U.S. military command centers. This improvement will allow crewmembers on mine hunting ships to send information to the centers more quickly.

In addition, the Navy is improving communication systems between mine hunting ships and other Navy ships. These systems will

The Navy continues to improve communication systems in its mine hunting ships.

allow *Inchon*'s crew to better communicate with mine hunting ship crews.

Other Improvements

The Navy is improving mine hunting ships in other ways. Researchers are working to improve the ships' sensors, computers, and remote control systems.

A plan called Assigned Countermeasures may further improve the Navy's mine hunting forces. Through this plan, other warships will be equipped with mine hunting gear. These ships then can avoid mines without support from MCMs or MHCs.

The Navy may equip submarines with Near-term and Long-term Mine Reconnaissance Systems. These systems include Unmanned Undersea Vehicles (UUVs). The UUVs will have sonar equipment to hunt for mines. Crewmembers will launch the UUVs through the submarines' torpedo tubes. These tubes on the subs' sides or top

The information center aboard mine hunting ships includes computers, monitors, and seats for the crew.

launch torpedoes. The submarines will help mine hunting ships locate and neutralize mines.

The Navy needs to keep all of its ships safe from mines. The Navy will probably continue to use MCMs and MHCs as its main mine hunting ships. New and improved equipment can make mine hunting ships even more important to the Navy.

MHCs will help keep the Navy's ships safe from mines in the future.

Words to Know

acoustic mine (uh-KOO-stik MINE)—a mine that senses a ship's sounds

bottom mine (BOT-uhm MINE)—a mine placed on the ocean floor

contact mine (KON-takt MINE)—a mine that explodes when an object hits it

degaussing system (dee-GAUS-ing SISS-tuhm)—a group of wires that creates electricity to cancel a ship's magnetism

moored mine (MORED MINE)—a mine attached to a cable that floats at a certain depth

neutralize (NOO-truh-lize)—to make a mine unable to harm a ship

pressure mine (PRESH-ur MINE)—a mine that senses the water pressure a ship creates

sonar (SOH-nar)—a device that uses sound waves to locate underwater objects

To Learn More

Butterfield, Moira. *Ships.* Look Inside Cross-Sections. New York: DK Publishing, 1994.

Green, Michael. *The United States Navy.* Serving Your Country. Mankato, Minn.: Capstone High-Interest Books, 1998.

MacKenzie, Lain. *The History of Warships.* The History Of. Hauppauge, New York: Barron's Educational Series, 1998.

Useful Addresses

Mine Warfare Command
325 Fifth Street SE
Corpus Christi, TX 78419

Naval Historical Center
805 Kidder Breese SE
Washington Navy Yard
Washington, DC 20374-5060

Naval Undersea Museum
610 Dowell Street
Keyport, WA 98345

Internet Sites

Mine Warfare Command
http://www.cnsl.spear.navy.mil/cmwc

Program Executive Office—Mine and Undersea Warfare
http://peomiw.navsea.navy.mil

The United States Navy
http://www.navy.mil

Index